W9-AAT-741

MY FIRST
JAPANESE
PHRASES

BY
JILL KALZ

ILLUSTRATED BY
DANIELE FABBRI

TRANSLATED BY
TRANSLATIONS.COM

This is my mother.
ぼく/わたしのおかあさんです。
(boku/watashi no okasān desu)

This is my aunt and uncle.
ぼく/わたしのおばさんとおじさんです。
(boku/watashi no obasan to ojisan desu)

PICTURE WINDOW BOOKS
a capstone imprint

TABLE OF
CONTENTS

HOW TO USE THIS DICTIONARY

This book is full of useful phrases in both English and Japanese. The English phrase appears first, followed by the Japanese phrase. Look below each Japanese phrase for help to sound it out. Try reading the phrases aloud.

Topic heading in English

Topic heading in Japanese

Additional phrases to learn

Phrase in English
Phrase in Japanese
(pronunciation)

NOTES ABOUT THE JAPANESE LANGUAGE

There are three systems for writing in Japanese: kanji, hiragana, and katakana. This book uses hiragana and some kanji and katakana. The hiragana characters appear in parentheses after the kanji characters.

There are 46 basic characters in hiragana. Two or more characters are placed next to each other to create a phrase.

In Japanese, personal pronouns are changed according to status and gender. For example, the word watashi is used for "me" by girls, and by all in formal settings. The word boku is used by boys, and by all in casual settings.

LETTERS OF THE ALPHABET
AND THEIR PRONUNCIATIONS

あ • ah

い • ee

う • oo

え • eh

お • oh

か • kah

き • kee

く • koo

け • keh

こ • koh

さ • sah

し • shee

す • soo

せ • seh

そ • soh

た • tah

ち • chee

つ • tsoo

て • teh

と • toh

な • nah

に • nee

ぬ • noo

ね • neh

の • noh

は • hah

ひ • hee

ふ • foo

へ • heh

ほ • hoh

ま • mah

み • mee

む • moo

め • meh

も • moh

や • yah

ゆ • yoo

よ • yoh

ら • rah

り • ree

る • roo

れ • reh

ろ • roh

わ • wa

を • oh

ん • n

IT SOUNDS *LIKE*

Romanji is the system of writing Japanese that spells out the sounds using Roman letters. In Romanji, there is no emphasis on syllables. A bar above the letters a, i, o, or u indicates a long vowel sound.

	SOUND	PRONUNCIATION	EXAMPLES	
CONSONANTS	b	like b in banana	bara	ba-ra
	d	like d in dog	desu	de-su
	g	like g in go	gohan	go-han
	h	like h in house	haru	ha-ru
	k	like k in kick	kirin	ki-rin
	m	like m in moon	mushi	mu-shi
	n	like n in now	namida	na-mida
	p	like p in pick	pinku	pin-ku
	r	like r in rock	risu	ri-su
	s	like s in smile; if followed by i, like she in she	semi shima	se-mi shi-ma
	t	like t in tap; if followed by i, like chi in chick; if followed by u, like ts in tsunami	tako chizu tsuki	ta-ko chi-zu tsu-ki
	w	like w in water	wa	wa
	y	like y in yogurt	yoru	yo-ru
	z	like z in zag; if followed by i, like gi in giraffe	zaru jishin	za-ru ji-shin
VOWELS	a	like u in lunch	asa	a-sa
	i	like ee in seek	inu	i-nu
	u	like oo in book	umi	u-mi
	e	like e in egg	eki	e-ki
	o	like o in on	oto	o-to
VOWEL COMBINATIONS	aa	like a in father	okaasan	o-kā-san
	ii	like ee in see	kuriimu	ku-rī-mu
	uu	like oo in school	kyuuri	kyū-ri
	ee	like a in say	oneesan	o-nē-san
	oo	like a in ball	otoosan	o-tō-san

English: THE BASICS

Japanese: 基本（きほん）(kihon)

Thank you.
ありがとうございます。
(arigatō gozaimasu)

You are welcome.
どういたしまして。
(dō itashimashite)

What is your name?
あなたのなまえは何（なん）ですか?
(anata no namae wa nan desu ka)

My name is___.
ぼく/わたしのなまえは___です。
(boku/watashi no namae wa___ desu)

MORE TO LEARN

Yes	No
はい	いいえ
(hai)	(iie)

Japanese: きもち (kimochi)

English: MEALS

Are you hungry?
あなたはおなかがすいていますか?
(anata wa onaka ga suite imasu ka)

I am hungry.
ぼく/わたしはおなかがすいています。
(boku/watashi wa onaka ga suite imasu)

thirsty
のどがかわいた。
(nodo ga kawaita)

What is for supper?
ばんごはんは何(なん)ですか?
(bangohan wa nan desu ka)

lunch
おひるごはん
(ohirugohan)

breakfast
あさごはん
(asagohan)

SPECIAL

MORE TO LEARN

I am not hungry.
ぼく/わたしはおなかがすいていません。
(boku/watashi wa onaka ga suite imasen)

Japanese: しょくじ (shokuji)

English: FAMILY

This is my mother.
ぼく/わたしのおかあさんです。
(boku/watashi no okāsan desu)

This is my aunt and uncle.
ぼく/わたしのおばさんとおじさんです。
(boku/watashi no obasan to ojisan desu)

my grandma and grandpa
ぼく/わたしのおばあちゃんとおじいちゃん。
(boku/watashi no obāchan to ojīchan)

Japanese: かぞく (kazoku)

Do you speak English?
あなたはえいごをはなしますか?
(anata wa eigo o hanashimasu ka)

French
フランスご
(furansu go)

German
ドイツご
(doitsu go)

Spanish
スペインご
(supein go)

Chinese
ちゅうごくご
(chūgoku go)

DUTY FREE

A little.
少(すこ)し。
(sukoshi)

MORE TO LEARN

father	older sister	younger sister	older brother	younger brother
おとうさん	おねえさん	いもうと	おにいさん	おとうと
(otōsan)	(onēsan)	(imōto)	(onīsan)	(otōto)

15

It is time to get up.
おきるじかんです。
(okiru jikan desu)

What time is it?
今(いま)何(なん)じですか?
(ima nanji desu ka)

It is time to go to bed.
ねるじかんです。
(neru jikan desu)

When are we leaving?
ぼくたち/わたしたちはいつしゅっぱつしますか?
(bokutachi/watashitachi wa itsu shuppatsu shimasu ka)

Japanese: ようびとじかん (yōbi to jikan)

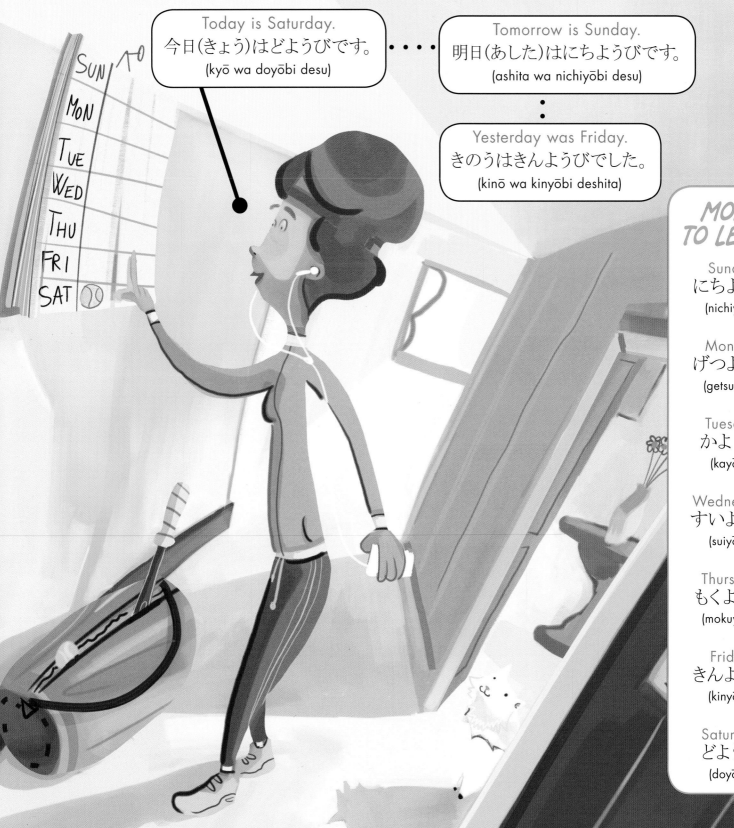

Today is Saturday.
今日(きょう)はどようびです。
(kyō wa doyōbi desu)

Tomorrow is Sunday.
明日(あした)はにちようびです。
(ashita wa nichiyōbi desu)

Yesterday was Friday.
きのうはきんようびでした。
(kinō wa kinyōbi deshita)

MORE TO LEARN

Sunday
にちようび
(nichiyōbi)

Monday
げつようび
(getsuyōbi)

Tuesday
かようび
(kayōbi)

Wednesday
すいようび
(suiyōbi)

Thursday
もくようび
(mokuyōbi)

Friday
きんようび
(kinyōbi)

Saturday
どようび
(doyōbi)

Japanese: 月（つき）ときせつ (tsuki to kisetsu)

I love summer!
ぼく/わたしはなつが大（だい）すきです！
(boku/watashi wa natsu ga daisuki desu)

fall
あき
(aki)

winter
ふゆ
(fuyu)

spring
はる
(haru)

How is the weather?
天気(てんき)はどうですか?
(tenki wa dō desu ka)

It is raining.
雨(あめ)です。
(ame desu)

snowing
ゆきがふっている
(yuki ga futte iru)

sunny
はれている
(harete iru)

Don't forget an umbrella!
かさをわすれないでください!
(kasa o wasurenaide kudasai)

Japanese: 天気（てんき）(tenki)

It is cold.
さむいです。
(samui desu)

It is hot.
あつい。
(atsui)

Wear a coat.
コートをきてください。
(kōto o kite kudasai)

hat
ぼうし
(bōshi)

mittens
てぶくろ
(tebukuro)

boots
ブーツ
(būtsu)

We study <u>science</u>.
ぼくたち/わたしたちはりかをべんきょうします。
(bokutachi/watashitachi wa ri ka o benkyō shimasu)

math
さんすう
(sansū)

history
れきし
(rekishi)

May I use your <u>pencil</u>?
あなたのえんぴつをつかってもいいですか?
(anata no enpitsu o tsukattemo ii desu ka)

your scissors
あなたのはさみ
(anata no hasami)

your glue
あなたののり
(anata no nori)

MORE TO LEARN

My teacher is___.
わたし/ぼくの先生(せんせい)は___です。
(watashi/boku no sensei wa ___ desu)

This is my favorite book!
これはぼく/わたしが一ばんすきな本(ほん)です!
(kore wa boku/watashi ga ichiban sukina hon desu)

Japanese: 学校（がっこう） (gakkō)

Where is the bathroom?
トイレはどこですか？
(toire wa doko desu ka)

lunchroom
しょくどう
(shokudō)

the bus stop
バスてい
(basutei)

Go right.
右（みぎ）に行（い）ってください。
(Migi ni itte kudasai)

left
ひだり
(hidari)

straight ahead
しょうめん
(shōmen)

Are you ready for the test?
テストのじゅんびはできていますか？
(tesuto no junbi wa dekite imasu ka)

I forgot.
わすれました。
(wasuremashita)

Japanese: いえ　(Ie)

What did you say?
あなたは何(なん)といいましたか?
(anata wa nan to iimashita ka)

Mom is in the garage.
おかあさんはしゃこにいます。
(okāsan wa shako ni imasu)

Go outside.
外(そと)に行(い)ってください。
(Soto ni itte kudasai)

upstairs
にかい
(nikai)

downstairs
いっかい
(ikkai)

Japanese:  しゅみ (shumi)

Numbers • すうじ (sūji)

1 one • 一（いち）(ichi)

2 two • 二（に）(ni)

3 three • 三（さん）(san)

4 four • 四（し）(shi)

5 five • 五（ご）(go)

6 six • 六（ろく）(roku)

7 seven • 七（しち）(shichi)

8 eight • 八（はち）(hachi)

9 nine • 九（きゅう）(kyū)

10 ten • 十（じゅう）(jū)

11 eleven • 十一（じゅういち）(jūichi)

12 twelve • 十二（じゅう）(jūni)

13 thirteen • 十三（じゅうさん）(jūsan)

14 fourteen • 十四（じゅうし）(jūshi)

15 fifteen • 十五（じゅうご）(jūgo)

16 sixteen • 十六（じゅうろく）(jūroku)

17 seventeen • 十七（じゅうしち）(jūshichi)

18 eighteen • 十八（じゅうはち）(jūhachi)

19 nineteen • 十九（じゅうきゅう）(jūkyu)

20 twenty • 二十（にじゅう）(nijū)

30 thirty • 三十（さんじゅう）(sanjū)

40 forty • 四十（よんじゅう）(yonjū)

50 fifty • 五十（ごじゅう）(gojū)

60 sixty • 六十（ろくじゅう）(rokujū)

70 seventy • 七十（ななじゅう）(nanajū)

80 eighty • 八十（はちじゅう）(hachijū)

90 nintey • 九十（きゅうじゅう）(kyūjū)

100 one hundred • 百（ひゃく）(hyaku)

COLORS・いろ (iro)

 red・**あか**
(aka)

 purple・**むらさき**
(murasaki)

 orange・**オレンジ**
(orenji)

 pink・**ピンク**
(pinku)

yellow・**きいろ**
(kiiro)

 brown・**ちゃいろ**
(chairo)

 green・**みどり**
(midori)

 black・**くろ**
(kuro)

 blue・**あお**
(ao)

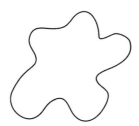 white・**しろ**
(shiro)

READ MORE

Kudela, Katy R. *My First Book of Japanese Words*. Bilingual Picture Dictionaries. Mankato, Minn.: Capstone Press, 2010.

Mahoney, Judy. *Teach Me—Everyday Japanese*. Teach Me—. Minnetonka, Minn.: Teach Me Tapes, 2008.

Sato, Anna, and Eriko Sato. *My First Japanese Kanji Book: Learning Kanji the Fun and Easy Way!* North Clarendon, Vt.: Tuttle Pub., 2009.

INTERNET SITES

FactHound offers a safe, fun way to find Internet sites related to this book. All of the sites on FactHound have been researched by our staff.

Here's all you do:

Visit *www.facthound.com*

Type in this code: 9781404875142

Check out projects, games and lots more at
www.capstonekids.com
Super-cool stuff!

LOOK FOR ALL THE BOOKS IN THE SPEAK ANOTHER LANGUAGE SERIES:

MY FIRST ARABIC *PHRASES*

MY FIRST FRENCH *PHRASES*

MY FIRST GERMAN *PHRASES*

MY FIRST ITALIAN *PHRASES*

MY FIRST JAPANESE *PHRASES*

MY FIRST MANDARIN CHINESE *PHRASES*

MY FIRST RUSSIAN *PHRASES*

MY FIRST SPANISH *PHRASES*

Thanks to our adviser for her expertise, research, and advice:
Yoko Hasegawa, Professor
Department of East Asian Languages and Cultures
University of California, Berkeley

Editor: Shelly Lyons
Set Designer: Alison Thiele
Production Designer: Eric Manske
Art Director: Nathan Gassman
Production Specialist: Laura Manthe
The illustrations in this book were created digitally.

Picture Window Books
1710 Roe Crest Drive
North Mankato, Minnesota 56003
877-845-8392
www.capstonepub.com

Library of Congress Cataloging-in-Publication Data
Kalz, Jill.
My first Japanese phrases / by Jill Kalz ; illustrations by Daniele Fabbri.
    p. cm. — (Capstone Picture Window books. Speak another language!)
  Text in both English and Japanese.
ISBN 978-1-4048-7514-2 (library binding)
ISBN 978-1-4048-7738-2 (paperback)
ISBN 978-1-4048-7997-3 (ebook PDF)
1. Japanese language—Textbooks for foreign speakers—English—Juvenile literature. 2. Japanese language—Conversation and phrase books—English—Juvenile literature. I. Fabbri, Daniele, ill. II. Title.
  PL539.3.K35 2013
  495.6'83421—dc23
                            2012003636

Summary: Simple text paired with themed illustrations invite the reader to learn to speak Japanese.

Printed in the United States of America in North Mankato, Minnesota.
042012   006682CGF12